Heroic Feats

Thrillogy

Edited by Paul Collins and Meredith Costain

sundance

Read all of the

 **Thrillogy** Titles

Published by Sundance Publishing
P.O. Box 1326, 234 Taylor Street, Littleton, MA 01460

Copyright in individual stories remains with the authors.

First published 1999 as Spinouts by
Addison Wesley Longman Australia Pty Limited
95 Coventry Street, South Melbourne 3205 Australia
Exclusive United States Distribution: Sundance Publishing

ISBN 0-7608-4828-9

Printed in Canada

Contents

The Drawing

OF IXT

The author
Andrew Chapman
talks about the story

"I wanted to capture elements of the stories of Jack Vance (a famous fantasy writer) and combine them with my favorite type of story—the secret gateway into other worlds."

The Drawing of Ixt

During the night, the warlock Kleg and his band of monstrous bird-creatures broke into the castle of the sorcerer Tharn. They slew everyone while they slept. Kleg had hoped to obtain a magical item that Tharn was said to possess. When Kleg could not find it amongst the overturned furniture and corpses in the castle, he raged up and down, tearing at his thick, black hair and beard with his bloodied hands.

"I risked my life to summon the demon that gave us the power of invisibility!" he roared. "Where is the gate to the dream world of Ixt? I must have it!"

The twelve, terrible bird-creatures watched him in silence. They were called renders, and their tiny, black eyes glistened under their low brows. Their naked, black talons twitched with the memory of the killing, but they waited patiently while their master ranted.

"Find it," he yelled at the renders, "find me the gate to Ixt! I must have Tharn's greatest treasure! Take the place apart, brick by brick. Find it! But be careful, for Tharn is known for his tricks and illusions."

The twelve crimson-skinned creatures sat hunched under the shadows of their massive, leathery wings. Then they stirred into action, tearing holes in the walls and knocking the floorboards and ceiling into matchsticks. While they worked, Kleg stamped heavily back and forth, muttering to himself. Occasionally he paused to watch the progress of the demolition and to shout instructions to his hulking slaves. "You've missed that corner, you fools! And over there I see a cabinet still standing. Take it apart. I must have the gate to Ixt."

Soon, the sounds of destruction began to fade and the clouds of dust settled. The renders returned to stand in a silent group around Kleg. To all sides, the castle lay in ruins. Only a few walls rose up from a sea of rubble and smashed furniture.

"Well?" Kleg said.

There was a pause. Then, the closest render hissed, "It is not here."

Kleg opened his mouth to scream in anger. But

he clicked it shut when he saw that one of the renders held a boy by the throat. The boy's face was almost hidden behind the creature's massive claws. He appeared to be about twelve years old.

"What do you have there?" Kleg asked.

The render inspected the boy, holding him up in one claw and almost choking him. The others watched with glistening eyes. "It is a boy," the render finally said.

Kleg's face turned red. "Why did you not tell me of him immediately?"

The render shrugged, flapping its wings. "You did not ask."

Kleg stepped forward, his black cloak swirling around his large body. "Give him to me."

"It has been days since we tasted live boy-flesh."

"What do I care about that!" Kleg gestured impatiently.

The render whined. "When will we eat?"

"When you find the gate to Ixt," Kleg snarled. He snatched the boy from the render's grasp. "Who are you? Tell me quickly now and speak the truth or the renders shall have you."

The boy had almost been crushed in the render's vice-like grip. He gasped for breath, almost unable to reply to Kleg's question. "I . . . I am called Quib. I make drawings for Tharn."

Kleg frowned in puzzlement. "Drawings? What do you draw?"

"Tharn would tell me of strange and far-off places. I would draw them."

Kleg thought hard. "To what purpose?" he said. "What was his interest in these drawings?"

Quib shrugged nervously. "Who can say? He would take the drawings into his chamber and there perform his magic upon them. He cared not how I drew but only that I drew with this." And he pulled forth a long piece of charcoal.

Kleg snatched it. "What is it?"

"It is from the dream world of Ixt."

A sharp breath escaped Kleg's lips. He turned the piece of charcoal this way and that, inspecting it, as if he thought it might suddenly transform itself into something else. For a moment he paused, thinking. Then he returned it to the boy. "Show me how you draw. And no trickery, or else you will know your fate."

Trembling with fear and keeping an eye on the silent renders, Quib wet the tip of the charcoal with his tongue. Then he began to draw upon a wall. Kleg watched him keenly. Here was the gate to Ixt, of that he was certain. Without knowing it, this boy would show him how to open it. Tharn's secrets would soon be his.

At first Quib drew a large border, three feet to a side. Then he began to draw lines within it. Kleg watched closely. Quib's hand was rough and unskilled like a child's. Kleg could make neither head nor tail of whatever it was that Quib was drawing. But then a detail leaped out, and Kleg could see that Quib was drawing a tree.

A most curious style, Kleg thought. No sooner had Quib begun one detail than he would ignore what he had done and start an entirely different part of the picture. In turn, this part would be left half done as he moved on to another part of the drawing.

Then Quib started working on the tree again. Kleg marveled that with a scratch here and a scratch there, Quib was able to make the tree look almost real. It seemed to develop depth, as if it were actually round and not flat. Kleg felt he could sense the trembling of the leaves upon its branches and feel the warm breeze stirring the leaves. Fascinated, he leaned forward to take a closer look, then reached out.

Remarkable! Not only did the tree look real, but it seemed to Kleg that he could almost feel the bark against his fingertips. Now he saw a narrow, dirt path next to the tree. It led down a slope toward a small village of tall houses with red roofs. Beyond that stood a line of jagged, gray mountains.

Some kind of festival was going on in the village. Townsfolk were crowded into the square. They seemed to be dancing. Frustratingly, the curve of the hill hid the details.

Without realizing it, Kleg had taken his hand off the tree and started down the slope toward the village. He could hear music now, sweet, yet somehow sad. Bright laughter lured him onward. Running now, he plunged into the crowd of dancing couples. The men wore blue smocks and the women had rainbow-colored ribbons in their hair.

Slowly, Kleg strolled, turning his head from side to side, marveling at everything he saw. As he stopped outside the inn, the smiling keeper emerged to bring him a jug of cool cider. But before he could take a sip, he was swept up by the crowd into their high-stepping dance. He was laughing as if he were in a dream.

A long time seemed to pass, filled with dancing and feasting. He suddenly thought that he should be getting back somewhere, but he couldn't quite remember where. There was something about a drawing . . . And now that he thought about it, he couldn't be exactly sure as to the way he had come. This side street? No, that was a dead end. How about this one? No, that was blocked, too. This one perhaps . . .

Suddenly he noticed that the sky had grown black as a nightmare. He spun around in panic. The villagers had vanished. Now through the empty streets he could hear something massive approaching. There was one heavy footfall after another—a sinister sound. Kleg staggered backward as a long, inhuman shadow came out from a nearby alley. Then he screamed.

Quib stepped back from the drawing and considered it for a moment. Then he rubbed it away with his sleeve, leaving only a dirty smudge upon the wall. Behind him the renders moved uneasily.

"Where has Kleg gone?" one said. "We are hungry."

Quib turned. He moved a hand over his face and to the renders it seemed that the boy had been replaced by a man. He looked with sorrow at the demolished house full of the bodies of the slain.

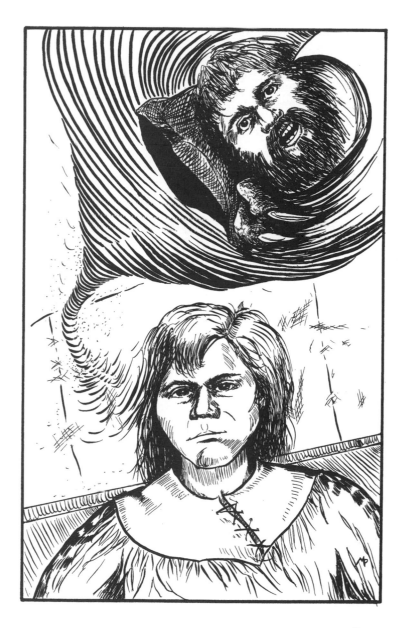

Then he glanced up at the renders with a severe expression.

"Kleg is gone. You are free of him. You may depart my house." Tharn turned and shuffled off into the wreckage to save what he could. The renders glanced at one another. Then, as if at a signal, they leaped wordlessly into the night sky. Wheeling away across the stars, they vanished into the west.

Over the Hills
and
Faraway

The author
Jenny Pausacker
talks about the story

"Being a writer is a little like doing jigsaw puzzles. Two things floated into my mind for this story—an image of a girl watching, while her friends were taken away; and the sentence, 'The mountains were higher than they looked on the map and the mines were deeper.' Then I worked out a way to fit them together in a classic fairy tale pattern."

Over the Hills and Faraway

Once there was a girl named Leah, who lived in a tiny village in a kingdom called Monetaria. On the first day of every month, the king's guards came tramping over the hills to round up all of the ten-year-old girls. Then, they took the girls to King Guilder's palace in Faraway.

They didn't take Leah, though. On the first day of the month after she turned ten, her mother dressed her in her brother's shirt and work pants and sent her off to the fields. Leah was digging a trench when the guards arrived. She leaned on her spade and watched while they herded her best friend, Hildy, down the road and over the hills.

Hildy cried, every step of the way.

Leah missed Hildy terribly. Still, as her other best friend, Joel, said, "There's a good side to everything." The schoolmaster didn't usually teach girls to read, but since Leah was the only girl left, she went to school with Joel and the other boys.

So many books! Schoolmaster had been thrown out of Faraway for arguing with the king, and he'd brought ten big, fat, leather-bound volumes with him, stuffed full of interesting facts. Every evening Joel and Leah would lie in the grass under the apple trees and talk about the things they'd learned.

How travelers had made maps of every road and mountain in Monetaria. How all of the eels in all of the rivers of the world swam to the Seaweed Sea to lay their eggs. How the dragons in their fairy tales were really big lizards called dinosaurs. There was nothing magical about them at all.

Then, as the stars started to glimmer through the leaves, they would talk about Hildy. She was still Leah's best friend, of course, and Joel had been in love with her ever since they were five years old. They were determined to bring her back home, and they knew exactly what to do.

King Guilder loved money. He'd found out that before a marriage, the boy's parents always paid a bride price to the girl's parents, so he collected all of the young girls. If the young men wanted to marry, they had to go to the big Wedding Fair in Faraway and bid for one of the girls. Half the bride price went to the girl's family, and the other half went to the king.

For seven years, Joel and Leah saved every penny they could. Then, a month before the Wedding Fair, Leah watched Joel ride away on his father's draft horse. Two months later, he came riding back again, alone.

"Hildy wasn't there," he told Leah. "The people in the town told me one girl always disappears, every year. They say . . . " He swallowed and tried again. "They say the king gives her to a dragon."

Leah frowned. "That's impossible. Remember what Schoolmaster said."

Joel wouldn't listen to her, though. He walked away and locked himself in his room. "Give up, Leah," he yelled when she banged on the door. "This time there's nothing we can do."

But Leah couldn't give up. Late that night, she sneaked into the kitchen and packed some food. Then she sneaked over to the schoolhouse and copied one of the maps from Schoolmaster's atlas.

And after that she swung her bag over her shoulder and set off to find Hildy.

The mountains were higher than they looked on the map, and the roads were longer. Leah climbed up ridges, slithered down cliffs, and followed dark tunnels through the rock and out the other side. A

cartload of traveling musicians gave her a ride across the plain and told her all about Faraway.

"It's on the edge of the Seaweed Sea," they said. "King Guilder's palace is covered in gold—gold paint on the walls, gold pillars, gold knives and forks. But the most amazing sight of all is the Temple of the Dragon, here in this valley outside the city."

The Temple of the Dragon? That sounded like a good place to start. Leah said good-bye to the musicians and scrambled down a slippery path beside a deep river. She had to watch her feet very carefully, so she was startled when she turned the last corner and glanced up to see a dragon's head looming over her.

Leah wanted to run but, just in time, she heard Schoolmaster's voice saying, "Dragons are fairy tales." She looked again and laughed. The dragon's head was just a huge cave in the side of the valley, with jagged rocks like teeth and boulders like bulging eyes.

She hurried past a little hut that had a large vegetable garden and walked into the cave. A thin line of light poked through the rocks at the far

end. Leah could see a flat, black pool, a strip of gravel curving around one side, and glints of gold sparkling on the opposite wall. But no dragons anywhere.

Then her foot slipped and a stone rolled into the pool.

The black surface churned. A blunt, narrow head reared up, splashing water all over her. The creature was huge and snakelike. It had a long, looped body, twisting and turning, that was as pale as the ash from last night's fire.

"The dragon!" Leah squealed and ran.

She hurtled out of the cave and bumped into a big man with golden eyes, a golden beard, and a gold brocade coat. Behind him stood five guards, a tall man wearing a dragon robe, and a pale, skinny boy in a dragon tunic, who was patting a young girl on the shoulder.

The girl was Hildy.

Leah thought so fast that her brain hurt. She wiped her wet face, licked river water off her fingers, and bowed to the big man. "You're King Guilder, aren't you, and you want the gold from the cave?" she guessed. "Well, I can get it for you, if you'll lend me your guards and a shovel."

King Guilder chuckled. "I know what you're thinking," he said. "But you're wrong. The dragon will never leave that cave, because dragons love gold even more than I do. That's why we feed a girl to it every year—so my miners can row over and chip some gold from the wall, while the dragon's sleeping off its snack." Then he polished his golden rings on his sleeve and added, "Still, the Priest of the Dragon has to say the dragon-ritual first. I'll let you borrow my guards for an hour."

The pale, skinny boy ran to fetch a shovel from the vegetable garden. Leah flashed a thumbs-up sign at Hildy and led the guards to the gap at the far end of the cave. While they heaved at the boulders, she dug a ditch in the gravel. She lifted out the last shovelful and jumped back as water rushed into the channel.

A creature with a blunt, narrow head rushed along with the water. It went tumbling through the gap in the rocks and speeding off down the river toward the Seaweed Sea.

Leah marched out of the cave and faced King Guilder. "That wasn't a dragon," she told him. "It was just a big old eel that wanted to go home."

The king's golden eyes sparkled. "Well done," he boomed. "You deserve a reward, my lad. I'll give you Hildy. I won't even make you pay a bride price for her."

Leah grinned to herself. King Guilder might be rich, but he was also stupid. He wouldn't listen when Schoolmaster argued with him about dragons and eels and all of those facts from his big, leather-bound books. And he couldn't see that she was actually a girl wearing her brother's work pants.

Still, at least she could take Hildy back to the village now. Except that, when she turned around, Hildy and the pale, skinny boy were clinging to each other tightly.

Leah watched them for a while, and then she sighed.

"I think Hildy would rather stay here," she said. "Faraway's her home now. It's time I went home as well."

The mountains seemed smaller than before, and the roads didn't seem as long. Leah spent the whole journey wondering how to tell Joel she'd failed. As she trudged along the path to the village, he came

running to meet her. She stared at her feet and muttered, "Hildy's not coming back from Faraway."

"But is she safe and happy?" Joel asked, and Leah nodded. He shrugged and said, "See? There's a good side to everything."

"Aren't you sorry?" Leah burst out. "After all, you spent the last seven years talking about Hildy."

"You could say that," he agreed. "Or you could say I spent the last seven years talking to you."

Leah thought about Hildy. She thought about all of the unknown girls who wouldn't be fed to the dragon. And finally she thought about Joel.

"Hmm," she said. "Maybe you're right. Maybe there is a good side to everything."

Return of Nakos

The author
Russell Blackford
talks about the story

"*Return of Nakos* is set in the thirteenth century, a fascinating period of history that most people know little about. At the time of action, the great city of Constantinople (also known as Byzantium) has been conquered by the Crusaders."

Russell Blackford

Return of Nakos

Zoarash was trapped!

The young Persian magician had traveled far. Dry desert stretched behind him, offering no place to run or hide. Three days before, he'd lost his magical sky boat in a battle with a gigantic sun bird. And he was forced to complete his quest on foot. He was alone. His giant hunting cat, Regulus, had gone in search of food for them.

In front of him flowed the mighty Euphrates River. From its waters reared a monstrous, bony-skulled creature, which waded ashore, then hopped forward jerkily. It was twice the height of a man, with teeth like daggers, a dozen green tentacles, and a long, scaly tail that curled over its back like a scorpion's sting. A pair of sharp, curved spikes stuck out from the tail on either side.

Zoarash drew his sword and struck at the creature's thick skull. The tentacles grew longer, reaching out to encircle him, as he tried to hack

free. And then, a new foe entered the fight. As Zoarash hacked and slashed, another power reached into his mind, searching for the knowledge it needed. Zoarash let this new enemy probe into a carefully prepared place in his mind, while he continued the fight.

Just as Zoarash managed to break free of the monster's tentacles, it turned its back and lashed at him with its spiked tail. His strength fading, Zoarash made one last lunge with his sword. But although it looked as though his sword had cut right through the monster's neck and shoulders, it felt like he had cut through air!

Zoarash jumped back as his enemy dissolved into gray smoke, then blew away on the wind.

The monster had been a trick. A magical illusion, sent to distract him so that the ancient sorcerer, Leo Nakos, could read his mind from afar. Yet, the monster had been solid when he was fighting it. Zoarash could easily have died.

Grimly, he shook his head. The sorcerer was playing with him. He would see about that.

The next morning, Zoarash had a full stomach and a partner in his quest. Regulus had returned.

Together, they made their way northward toward the mountains.

Regulus was a huge panther, the size of a bull. Magicians from faraway had bred his kind over hundreds of years. He had a coat of thick, blue-black fur with a sheen like a raven's wings. The hunting cat was smarter than some humans. He could kill any animal and outrun most.

Like others trained in the magic of his homeland, Zoarash could fly, although only for short distances. Once he was close to the desert fortress of Nakos, he would fly the rest of the way.

Forty years before, Nakos had stolen the lost sword of Attila from its hiding place in the treasury of Byzantium. It was that great city's most important secret, for the sword held incredible powers. It was said that whichever kingdom or empire possessed it would never be conquered by its enemies.

For centuries, Byzantium was unconquered. But now, Nakos had the sword, and the city had fallen to invaders from the West. The Byzantine rulers were banished.

Ten days ago, Zoarash had appeared magically to the Byzantine rulers, informing them that he could find the lost sword. But the proud noblemen had mocked him. "You are but a beardless boy," they jeered. "Begone, before we lose our patience!"

Well, thought Zoarash, as he began the long walk toward Nakos's mountain fortress, he would show them what he was made of. He would return with the sword. Zoarash was a true warrior-magician trained in a magical tradition thousands of years old.

He would deal with Nakos and make him see reason or face the consequences. Zoarash was ready for a battle of magic.

Days passed, and they were almost there. A dark brown vulture flew overhead. It traced huge circles against the sky, watching the pair curiously. "Nakos's spy," Zoarash said to Regulus. He smiled at the big cat's scowl.

Zoarash used his magical strength to lift himself into the sky. Regulus followed him. The vulture squawked at them, then soared away.

Into the mountains Zoarash and Regulus flew. There, on a high outcrop of rock, stood the fortress of Leo Nakos. Zoarash and the hunting cat descended, landing in a barren courtyard.

There was a flash of blinding light that made Zoarash shut his eyes. Regulus squealed. The young Persian opened his eyes just in time to see the terrible figure of Nakos stride into the yard.

The Byzantine sorcerer was so old that only his magic held him together. Yet, he was an awesome sight. He was taller than any normal man and built like a tower of iron. His long hair and curly beard were jet black, but his skin seemed bleached white. He wore a round helmet and a suit of chain-mail armor that fell to his ankles.

Nakos started to draw a curved weapon from its scabbard. "You seek the lost sword of Attila?" he asked. "You must know that I will never give it up."

"You have triumphed," Zoarash said. "Byzantium has fallen to its enemies. Many of its rulers are dead, and the rest are in exile."

"Yes," said Nakos. "That is how I planned it."

"The Byzantines need the lost sword," Zoarash said. "You must return it to them. Otherwise, they can never recapture their city."

Nakos laughed. "Why should I care? As long as they suffer, I have my revenge!"

"Revenge cannot last forever."

"Listen, boy," Nakos said, "I served Byzantium faithfully. Yet I was accused of treason. That's what the city was like, full of evil schemes."

"I know that," Zoarash argued. "But the ones who betrayed you are now dead. Those who remain will welcome you. They need your help, you and the lost sword. You must return. You will be rewarded."

"Rewarded? Ha!" Nakos's voice thundered. "Let them all crawl on the earth until their doom. Their fathers should never have turned against me."

"Is your anger really so deep?" Zoarash asked.

"Yes!" Nakos glared at the young magician. "It is deeper than any well, deeper than any sea. Nothing will end my fury at the Byzantines. Nothing."

"Then we must be enemies," Zoarash challenged.

In some ways, he felt sorry for Nakos. He knew that the Byzantine rulers could be proud and cruel. Nakos was right. Many good people had been tricked and ruined. They said that the great city had been evil and had deserved its fate.

As Zoarash pondered this, Nakos seemed to grow even taller, like a mountain of living metal. "My anger gives me strength," he said. "It makes me invincible."

"No one is invincible," said Zoarash.

"Ha! You are but a mere boy. You haven't seen my power, little apprentice."

"I'm a full-fledged warrior-magician," Zoarash said proudly.

"Very well. But I have opened your mind and read what is in there. I know all of your weaknesses. I know what you fear most."

"You think you do," Zoarash said.

Regulus tensed to spring at Nakos, but the Byzantine sorcerer just smiled and waved his hand lazily. The hunting cat fell down in a sprawl of black limbs, fast asleep. "So much for your companion," Nakos said as Regulus snored peacefully. "Now we are equally matched."

Then, before Zoarash could even draw his sword, Nakos said the single word, "*Fire!*"

He raised his hands. Sheets of flame leaped from his palms, seeming to consume the air all around them.

"*Fire!*" he cried again, gleefully. "I read in your mind that you fear fire more than anything else."

Yet the flames passed by Zoarash harmlessly.

"*Fire!*" Nakos said, yet again.

"Yes," Zoarash said. "The fire of your anger. Pour it out at me, good Leo Nakos. You have been terribly wronged. Give me all of your anger."

By now, Nakos should have realized that Zoarash had prepared himself for exactly this event. The warrior-magician had made himself immune to magical fire. But Nakos was so carried away by his anger, his hunger for revenge, that he continued the attack. More and more sheets of fire blew forth from his palms.

Zoarash had let Nakos see only part of his mind — the part that he'd chosen to reveal. What the Byzantine sorcerer had found there was a kind of illusion, like the tentacled monster, like all things created by magic.

The swirling fire was also an illusion. While it lasted, the magical fire could burn like ordinary flames, yet it was not real. Zoarash was ready for this, and he let it flow past him.

"Let it out," Zoarash said, "all of your fire, all of your anger. Let it out, Nakos. It will be better that way."

"Yes," Nakos said, as if starting to understand what was happening.

Finally, Nakos appeared to go out, like a candle that had been snuffed. He gazed at his hands as if puzzled.

"That's enough," Zoarash said. "Try no more. It's all over for you, Leo."

The huge Byzantine sorcerer toppled over like a fallen statue. In his heavy iron armor, he crashed with a *thud* to the stony ground. Zoarash ran to him. The old sorcerer's hair and beard had turned white, but his heart was beating. He would live, but he'd need help to restore his body and his troubled mind.

Zoarash unsheathed the long lost sword of Attila from its scabbard. Nakos would return to his people, but the sword would go with the young Persian.

As Zoarash stood, admiring the powerful weapon's beautiful, curved blade, Regulus opened his eyes. The huge, black animal stretched, like any cat after a long sleep.

Zoarash reached down to cuff the panther's head. "So you've come back, my friend." He smiled into the distance. "So ends our quest. I wonder what tomorrow will bring."

About the Illustrators

The Story Illustrator
Marianne Plumridge

Marianne Plumridge lives in Rhode Island with her husband, Bob Eggleton, who is also an illustrator. They share their home with approximately 1,000 Godzilla monsters and hundreds of dinosaurs, toys, and other odd beasties and creatures. The rest of their house is occupied by numerous books, paintings, art materials, and CDs, which help to keep her inspired.

The Cover Illustrator
Marc McBride

Marc McBride has illustrated covers for several magazines and children's books. Marc currently creates the realistic images for his covers using acrylic ink with an airbrush. To solve his messy studio problem, he plans to use computer graphics instead.